T0083136

Dances of Time

Bob Chilcott

for SATB chorus and piano or orchestra

Contents

1. Pastime with good company 3
2. Today 7
3. Gather ye rosebuds 13
4. To every thing there is a season 18
5. Life has loveliness to sell 27

MUSIC DEPARTMENT

OXFORD
UNIVERSITY PRESS

Composer's note

I am very fortunate to have known Brian Kay for almost all my life, since being a chorister at King's College, Cambridge, while he was a bass choral scholar. Brian has had a fruitful life working in the world of music, particularly excelling in the encouragement and development of amateur choir singing. When Brian and the Leith Hill Musical Festival asked me to write a piece in celebration of his twentieth season as Festival Conductor, the key thing for me was to find the right texts for the occasion. I decided to look for texts that reflected not only Brian's spirit but also the idea that, despite the passing of time, music and singing can help us to live in and celebrate the present. The first of the five texts, by King Henry VIII, tells of the joy of good company and friends. The second, by Thomas Carlyle, reflects in a wistful but positive way on the hope of the new day. Robert Herrick's 'Gather ye rosebuds' is a plea to us all to live life in the moment and not to procrastinate! In the fourth movement, verses from Ecclesiastes remind us that with the passing of time comes not only thankfulness, but also reflection and hope for the future. The piece ends with a setting of a poem by Sara Teasdale that brims with energy and positivity, and includes perhaps one of the most powerful mantras for choir singers and lovers of good life: 'For one white singing hour of peace count many a year of strife well lost.'

Duration: *c.*15 minutes

An accompaniment for orchestra (2 fl, 2 ob, 2 cl, 2 bsn, 2 hn, 2 tpt, timp, 2 perc, str) is available on hire/rental from the publisher or appropriate agent.

OXFORD
UNIVERSITY PRESS

Great Clarendon Street, Oxford OX2 6DP,
United Kingdom

© Oxford University Press 2015

Bob Chilcott has asserted his right under the Copyright, Designs and Patents Act, 1988, to be identified as the Composer of this Work

First published 2015

All rights reserved. No part of this publication may be reproduced, stored in a retrieval system, or transmitted, in any form or by any means, without the prior permission in writing of Oxford University Press

Permission to perform this work in public (except in the course of divine worship) should normally be obtained from a local performing right licensing organization, unless the owner or the occupier of the premises being used already holds a licence from such an organization. Likewise, permission to make and exploit a recording of this work should be obtained from a local mechanical copyright licensing organization

Enquiries concerning reproduction outside the scope of the above should be directed to the Music Rights Department, Oxford University Press, at music.permissions.uk@oup.com or at the address above

ISBN 978-0-19-340060-3

Music origination by Katie Johnston
Printed in Great Britain on acid-free paper by Halstan & Co. Ltd, Amersham, Bucks.

for Brian Kay and the choirs of the Leith Hill Musical Festival

Dances of Time

BOB CHILCOTT

1. Pastime with good company

King Henry VIII (1491–1547)

© Oxford University Press 2015

Printed in Great Britain

OXFORD UNIVERSITY PRESS, MUSIC DEPARTMENT, GREAT CLARENDON STREET, OXFORD OX2 6DP

The Moral Rights of the Composer have been asserted. Photocopying this copyright material is ILLEGAL.

13
heart is set: All good - ly sport for my com-fort, who shall me
18
S.
A.
let? Some dal - li - ance,
f
T.
B.
Youth must have some dal - li-ance, of good or ill some
23
some pas - tance; me-thinks then best, best: For
pas - tance; Com - pa-ny me-thinks then best, All thoughts and fan - cies to di-gest: For

28
i - dle - ness is chief mis - tress of vi - ces all. Then
32
ff
who can say but mirth and play is best of all?
ff
ff
37
Com - pa - ny with ho - nest - y is vir - tue, vi - ces to flee;

41
Com - pa - ny is good and ill but ev - 'ry man hath his free will. The
45
best en - sue, the worst es - chew, my mind shall be: Vir - tue to use, vice
f
f
f
50
to re - fuse, thus shall I use me.
ff
fff

2. *Today*

Thomas Carlyle (1795–1881)

9
use - less a - way.
Out of E - ter - ni - ty This
use - less a - way, a - way.
use - less a - way, a - way.
use - less a - way.
13
new Day is born;
In - to E - ter - ni - ty, At night, will re - turn, re -
mf ma dolce
In - to E - ter - ni - ty, At night, will re - turn, re -
In - to E - ter - ni - ty, At night, will re - turn, re -
In - to E - ter - ni - ty, At night, will re - turn, re -
p
mf ma dolce

16
mp
p
- turn, re - turn.
- turn, re - turn, re - turn.
- turn, re - turn, re - turn.
- turn, re - turn, re - turn.
3
20
p cresc.
So
So
So
p
cresc.
Be - hold it a - fore - time No eye ev - er did; So

23
f
mf dim.
soon it for ev - er from all eyes is hid, is hid, from all eyes is
soon it for ev - er from all eyes is hid, is hid, hid,
soon it for ev - er from all eyes is hid, is hid, hid,
soon it for ev - er from all eyes is hid, is hid, hid,
cresc.

27
p
p dolce
hid. So here hath been dawn - ing A - no-ther, a - no-ther blue
hid. So here hath been dawn - ing, dawn - ing A - no - ther, a -
hid. So here hath been dawn - ing, dawn - ing A - no-ther blue
hid. So here hath been dawn - ing, dawn - ing A - no-ther blue

31
mp espress.
Day, blue Day, blue Day, a - no-ther blue Day, a - no-ther
mp espress.
- no-ther blue Day, blue Day, Day, blue Day, a -
mp espress.
Day, blue Day, blue Day, a - no - ther, a -
mf
ma dolce
mp espress.
Day, blue Day, a -
mp espress.
35
mf ma dolce
p
blue Day, a - no-ther, a - no-ther blue Day, a - no-ther blue Day, a - no-ther
mf ma dolce
p
- no - ther blue Day, blue, blue Day, blue Day, a -
mf ma dolce
p
- no - ther blue Day, blue Day, a - no - ther, a -
p
mp
- no - ther blue Day, blue Day, a -
mf ma dolce
p

39
mp
blue Day, a - no - ther, a - no - ther blue Day,
mp
-no - ther blue Day, blue, blue Day,
mp
-no - ther blue Day, blue Day,
-no - ther blue Day, blue Day,
mp
42
p
blue Day, blue, blue Day.
p
blue Day, blue Day.
p
blue Day, blue, blue Day.
p
blue Day, blue Day.
rit.
rit.
p
pp

3. *Gather ye rosebuds*

Robert Herrick (1591–1674)

19
this same flow'r that smiles to - day To - mor - row will be
24
p
dy - ing, dy - ing.
p
29
f
S.
A.
The glo - rious lamp of heav'n, the sun, The high - er he's a - get - ting, The
T.
B.
f
f

34
ff
soon - er will his race be run, And near - er he's to set - ting. That age is best which
ff
ff
39
is the first, When youth and blood are warm - er; But be - ing spent, the worse, and worst Times
44
dim.
f dim.
still suc - ceed the for - mer, the for - mer,
dim.
f dim.
dim.
f dim.

48
mf
p
the for - mer.
mf
p
mf dim.
53
p
59
S.
A.
p
Then be not coy, but
64
use your time, And while ye may, go mar - ry:

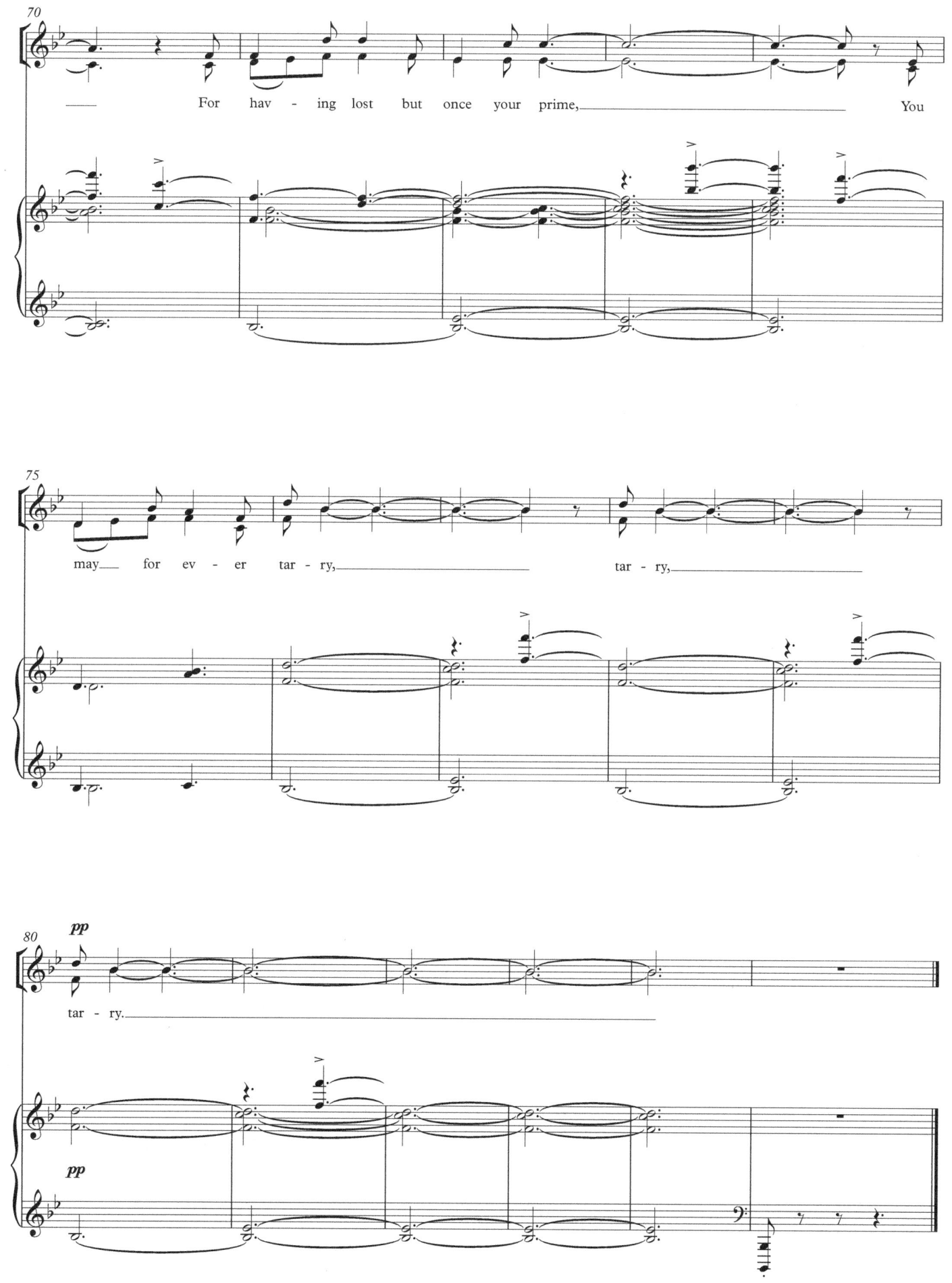
70
For hav - ing lost but once your prime, You
75
may for ev - er tar - ry, tar - ry,
80
pp
tar - ry.
pp

4. To every thing there is a season

Ecclesiastes 3: 1–8

15
mf ma dolce
sea - son, And a time to ev - 'ry pur - pose un - der the hea - ven,
mf ma dolce
mf ma dolce
19
p
hea - ven:
p
p
S./A. unis.
A little faster ♩ = c.80
A time to be born, and a
A little faster ♩ = c.80
24
time to die; A time to plant, and a time to pluck up
cresc.
cresc.

29
S./A.
T.
B.
mp
S.
A.
p
mp
that which is plant - ed, plant - ed; A
mp
mp
p
35
time to kill, and a time to heal;
mf unis.
time, a time to heal; A
mp
40
mf
A time to break down, and a time to build up;
mp
A
T.
B.
time to break down, and a time to build up;
mp
mf
mp

45
mf
time to weep, and a time to laugh; A
mf
mf
49
time to
f
time to mourn, and a time, a time to
f
f
53
p
dance;
p
p

57
BASSES p
B.
A time to cast a - way
62
stones, and a time to ga - ther stones to - ge - - ther;
68
mp
S.
A.
A time to em - brace, and a time to re - frain from em -
(B.)
T.
B.
T.
B.
mp
mp

73
mf
p
S./A. unis. p dolce
- brac - - ing;
A time to
mf
p
mf
p
78
mp
get, and a time to lose; A time to keep, and a time to cast a - way;
A time to
T./B. unis.
mp
dolce
83
time
mf
S.
A.
rend, and a time to sew; A time to keep si - lence, and a time, a time, a
T.
B.
mf
mp
mf

88
to speak,
f
time to speak,
A
time, a time to speak,
to speak;
f
time, a time
A time to
93
love, and a time of peace,
time to love, to love, a time of peace, a
love, and a time to hate; A time of war, and a time of peace, of
f
of peace, a time of peace,
98
dim.
mf dim.
time of
peace, peace, a time of peace, a time of
dim.
mf dim.
peace, a time of peace, a
dim.
mf dim.

103
rit.
time of
peace,
peace.
peace, of peace,
time of peace,
rit.
mp dim.
110
Tempo primo ♩ = c.63
Tempo primo ♩ = c.63
p dolce
114
p
poco cresc.
To ev - 'ry thing there is a
p
poco cresc.
p
poco cresc.

118
mp
sea - son, And a time to ev - 'ry pur - pose un - der the hea - ven,
mp
mp
122
p
hea - ven, hea - - - ven,
p
p
126
rit.
pp
hea - - - ven, hea - - ven.
pp
rit.
pp

5. *Life has loveliness to sell*

Sara Teasdale (1884–1933)

13
Soar - ing fire that sways and sings, And child - ren's fa - ces
17
look - ing up, Hold - ing won - der in a cup.
21
mf
Life has love - li - ness to sell,
mf
mf

26
espress.
Mu - sic like a curve of gold, Scent of pine trees
espress.
espress.
31
in the rain, Eyes that love you, arms that hold, And
35
f
for your spi - rit's still de - light, Ho - ly thoughts that star the
f
f

39
mp
night.
mp
mp
43
mp
mf
Spend all you have for love - li - ness, Buy it and ne - ver count the
mp
mf
mf
46
cost; For one white sing - ing hour of peace Count

strife well lost,
50
ma - ny a year of strife well lost,
53
f
And for a breath of ec - sta - sy Give all you have been, or could be, give
And for a breath of ec - sta - sy Give all you have been, or could be,
And for a breath of ec - sta - sy Give all you have been, or could be,
And for a breath of ec - sta - sy Give all you have been, or could be,

57
all you have been, or could be, give all you have been, or could be, could
give all, or could be, give all, or could be, could
give all you have been, or could be, give all you have been, or could
give all, or could be, give all, or could be,
61
ff
molto rit.
be, could be, could be.
be, could be, could be.
be, could be, could be.
be, could be, could be.
molto rit.
ff